Animal Helpers

by Robert R. O Brien
illustrated by Leslie Evans

Harcourt

Orlando   Boston   Dallas   Chicago   San Diego

Visit *The Learning Site!*

www.harcourtschool.com

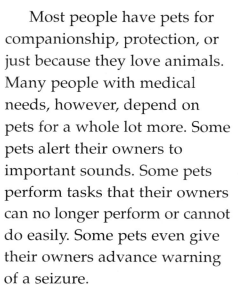

Most people have pets for companionship, protection, or just because they love animals. Many people with medical needs, however, depend on pets for a whole lot more. Some pets alert their owners to important sounds. Some pets perform tasks that their owners can no longer perform or cannot do easily. Some pets even give their owners advance warning of a seizure.

Everybody is familiar with dogs that help the blind, but there are all sorts of people that dogs help. Furthermore, dogs are not the only type of animal that helps people. Monkeys and horses are also used.

By far the most common animal helper is people's best friend. One of the programs that promote the use of dogs in therapy and assistance is Canine Companions for Independence, or CCI. The organization was founded in 1975 in Santa Rosa, California.

The people who started CCI and other similar programs realized that individuals with disabilities do not want to be dependent on other people. They want to be in control of as much of their own lives as possible. With a little assistance, they can get along just fine. The CCI programs provided ways of giving that assistance with the help of a four-legged companion.

Since the program started, volunteers all over the country have helped to train dogs. Hundreds of dogs have been placed in homes to help people get through their day by performing tasks like fetching things, opening doors, carrying backpacks, and even doing laundry!

The process starts with a puppy. Volunteer puppy raisers give a home to a Labrador or a golden retriever. These volunteers promise to care for and train the puppy for sixteen months. The puppy raisers have to care for and love the dog as if it were their very own dog to keep.

During that time, the puppy has to learn all the skills for being out in the world. The volunteer has to house-train the puppy, as well as train it to obey some simple commands. The puppy also learns how to behave in homes and with strangers of all ages, from children to elderly people.

Many puppy trainers take their dogs to their workplace to teach them how to deal with busy environments without getting in the way. They also include the dogs in other everyday activities, such as meetings, medical appointments, and visits to people in elder care centers.

After the initial training, the puppy goes to CCI school to learn how to be an assistance animal. First, the dog is checked to make sure it is healthy enough and friendly enough to fit in the program. Dogs who do not pass this initial screening become regular family pets.

Dogs that qualify then begin the serious training. The first part of the program lasts three months. The dog learns how to act around wheelchairs, and learns how to fetch, or retrieve, all kinds of items. To make sure the dog will be able to act properly around people in different situations, it is checked often for signs of temperamental behavior.

The next phase of the training also takes three months. During this period, the dog learns how to operate light switches and open and close doors. The dog continues to get experience in different real-life situations. The literature that CCI uses to describe this process states pointedly, "The dogs are screened to see if they truly have what it takes to become a CCI assistance dog. The dogs can be released at any time."

The training is very intense because the stakes are high. People are going to depend on these dogs for help in their daily lives. The dogs must be able to perform their tasks without fail.

During the next phase of the training, the dog and the new owner work together. For this two-week period, the dog and the new owner have a chance to get to know each other's needs and to learn to trust each other. This is called Team Training, because the dog and the new owner have to practice teamwork.

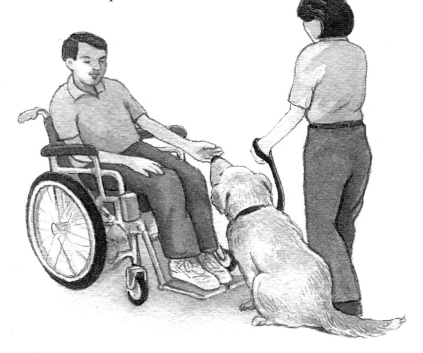

The owner has to learn how to care for and train the dog. The dog has to learn how to work with the owner. If dog and owner can work together properly, they graduate from the class. At a graduation ceremony the dog's trainer passes the leash to the new owner to show that the dog and the person are now a team.

Dogs help people in all sorts of ways. One way that is unusual is alerting people to seizures. People who have a medical condition called epilepsy have to take medication to prevent seizures. When a dog senses that its owner is about to have a seizure, the dog can alert him or her that it is time to take medicine.

Another disease that dogs can help with is Parkinson's disease. People with this disease sometimes "freeze" their legs. For example, when people with this illness are walking, their legs may suddenly stop moving. Dogs trained to help can nudge their feet and get them walking again. Dogs can also help people with this disease to stand up when they have fallen.

Of course, dogs are not the only kind of animal helper. Another amazing animal helper is the monkey.

Take a moment now to imagine your life if you were to lose the use of your arms and legs. Instead of being able to do all the things you normally do, like walk, play, and run, you would have to use a wheelchair. You would not be able to feed yourself, pick up something you needed, turn on a light, or dress yourself. You would depend on others to help you and to care for you.

Many advances have been made in assisting people who have to spend most of their day in wheelchairs. For instance, there are all kinds of electronic and computer-aided devices that help. There are some things, however, that a computer cannot do. That is where monkeys can help.

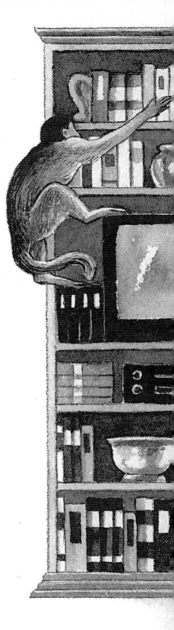

Capuchin monkeys, also called "organ grinder" monkeys, are originally from the tropical forests of Central and South America. These agile monkeys are about twelve to twenty-two inches long. Because of their great intelligence, they can be trained to do small tasks that give someone who uses a wheelchair greater independence.

Often people in wheelchairs are alone for many hours each day. Monkey helpers can stay with them to perform simple everyday tasks, such as turning the lights on and off, getting something to eat or drink, picking up dropped items, and assisting with books, tape recorders, or VCRs. With the helping hands of a monkey, people in wheelchairs can do things they would otherwise wait to have someone else do for them.

Being a monkey trainer is a lot of work. In some ways it can be very much like bringing up a baby. One difference is that a four-month-old baby cannot climb the curtains and swing on them!

There are very strict guidelines for being a monkey "foster parent." You cannot work out of your home. You cannot have children under the age of ten in the house. (Young children require a lot of attention, and so does a monkey. Both in one house would be too much.) You have to show that you are teaching the monkey good habits and giving it healthful meals, regular baths, and plenty of affection. A foster parent even has to buy or build a special cage for the monkey to stay in.

Monkeys are very curious, and they like to explore. You probably know that parents of small children have to "child-proof" their homes. Foster parents of monkey helpers have to "monkeyproof" their homes, which is much more difficult. Monkeys can reach and open things that a toddler could never get near. It is a lot of work and a lot of responsibility to be a monkey foster parent.

12

Once the monkey helper reaches a certain age and skill level, it starts going to the Training Center for classes. The classes meet four or five times a week and last for about forty-five minutes each. To learn to do the tasks they will have to perform, most monkeys need about a year of classes.

Once the monkey finishes its classes, it is paired up with someone who needs assistance. The needs of the individual are matched with the skills of the monkey.

The hardest part for the volunteers who raise and train the monkeys is giving them up. Still, the monkeys need to disengage from their foster parents so they can become devoted to their new owners.

13

Of course, horses have helped people since humans first figured out how to harness them. Many horses, such as police horses, have been retired from their work, but they find a new purpose as therapy animals.

Despite their huge bulk, most horses are gentle animals. Riders all over the world have discovered that people of all ages can benefit from riding and caring for horses.

For some, especially young children with special needs, the big animals offer huge enjoyment. The children love to do all the chores that horses require, such as grooming and feeding them. Doing these chores gives children a sense of accomplishment. When a child with special needs climbs up into the saddle and watches the horse snort, paw the ground, and then respond to a tug on the reins, that child feels great.

There are many horse helper programs around the world. The first therapeutic horse programs resembled formal horse training camps. Later, as therapists learned more about how to use horses to help people with special needs, programs changed to meet those needs.

These days, horses are used in programs to help children who have difficulty communicating or who have other kinds of problems with balance or muscle control. Therapists who treat these problems have noticed that the rhythm of the horse's movement helps focus the rider's attention on his or her own muscles and movements. Horse-riding stimulates the rider's muscles and helps his or her brain to connect feelings and movements. For children with severe language difficulties, riding is an experience that gets them to communicate more.

Working with an animal helper has so many benefits. These animals make people feel good. They help people with special needs achieve a level of independence they might not otherwise have. Caring for these talented animals gives their owners a sense of satisfaction, too.

Most of all, these animals and the people they help form a bond, or connection. The teamwork they share produces a friendship and a love that may be the most helpful and healing thing of all.